WRITING THE
U.S. CONSTITUTION

BY MATT BOWERS

SEQUENCE

AMICUS | AMICUS INK

Jw
342.73
BOW

Sequence is published by Amicus and Amicus Ink
P.O. Box 1329, Mankato, MN 56002
www.amicuspublishing.us

Library of Congress Cataloging-in-Publication Data
Names: Bowers, Matt, author.
Title: Writing the U.S. Constitution / by Matt Bowers.
Description: Mankato, Minnesota : Amicus, [2020] | Series: Sequence American government | Includes index. | Audience: Grades K-3.
Identifiers: LCCN 2018043281 (print) | LCCN 2018044887 (ebook) | ISBN 9781681517575 (pdf) | ISBN 9781681516752 (library binding) | ISBN 9781681524610 (pbk.)
Subjects: LCSH: United States. Constitution--Juvenile literature. | United States--Politics and government--1775-1783--Juvenile literature. | United States--Politics and government--1783-1789--Juvenile literature. | Constitutional history--United States--Juvenile literature.
Classification: LCC E303 (ebook) | LCC E303 .B785 2020 (print) | DDC 342.7302/9--dc23
LC record available at https://lccn.loc.gov/2018043281

Editor: Alissa Thielges
Designer: Veronica Scott
Photo Researcher: Holly Young

Photo Credits: Shutterstock/Baimieng cover; Shutterstock/Sascha Burkard cover; Shutterstock/Vizual Studio 5; Alamy/North Wind Picture Archives 6, 10–11, 18; WikiCommons/Wmpetro 9; Bridgeman Images/Rob Wood 13; Getty/American School 14–15; iStock/JPLDesigns 17; Shutterstock/Everett – Art 17; WikiCommons/Howard Chandler Christy 20–21; Superstock/3LH 22; Getty/Bettmann 24–25; Bridgeman Images/Universal History Archive, UIG 26; Getty/Marvin Joseph, The Washington Post 28–29

Printed in the United States of America

HC 10 9 8 7 6 5 4 3 2 1
PB 10 9 8 7 6 5 4 3 2 1

TABLE OF CONTENTS

The Constitution 4

A Weak Central Government 7

Writing the Constitution 12

Off to the States 23

Making Changes 27

■ ■ ■ ■ ■

Glossary 30

Read More 31

Websites 31

Index 32

The Constitution

Do you know what is the highest law of the United States? Here are some hints. It was written in 1787. It created the branches of government. And it protects the rights of the American people. Answer: the U.S. Constitution! This powerful document is old. But we still follow it every day. Its words have shaped our nation.

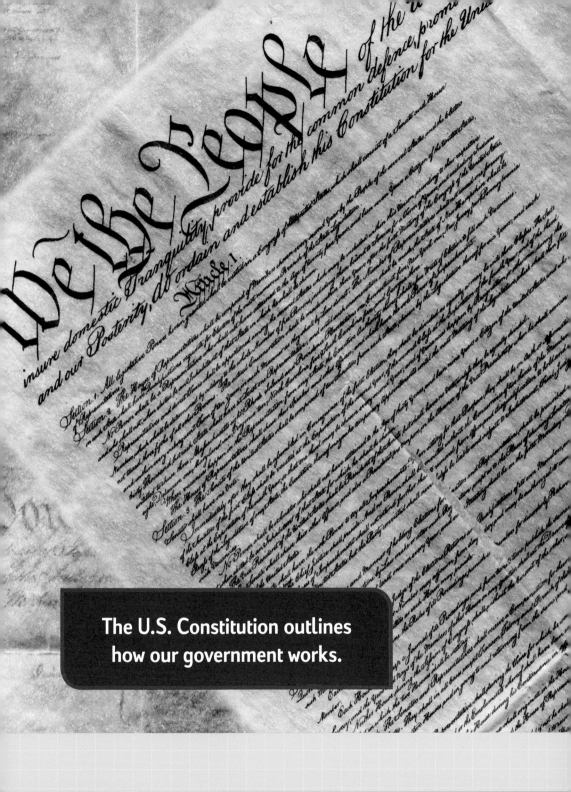

The U.S. Constitution outlines how our government works.

LOADING..LOADING..LOADING...

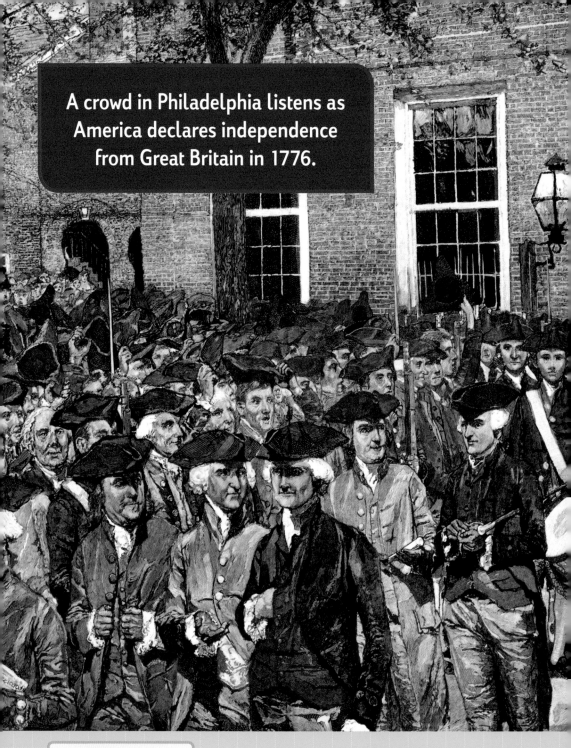

A crowd in Philadelphia listens as America declares independence from Great Britain in 1776.

The Articles of Confederation create a weak central government.

1781

LOADING . . . LOADING . . .

A Weak Central Government

In 1776, America had just split from Great Britain. It was a new nation. The states needed a central government. In 1781, the Articles of Confederation were approved. This united the states under a national government. But the government had very little power. It couldn't make the states pay taxes. There was no president. And it was hard to pass a law.

The government was weak for a reason. The states feared a central power with too much control. But a weak government was a problem, too. In 1786, rebels rose up. These people owed the government a lot of money. Rather than pay, they rebelled. They fought those who would take away their land. The central government couldn't stop them. A private army ended the rebellions in 1787.

A rebel, refusing to pay his taxes, takes down a tax collector.

The Articles of Confederation create a weak central government.

1781   1786–1787   NG . . . LOADING . . .

Weak central government can't stop rebellions.

The Articles of
Confederation create a
weak central government.

Leaders from states meet
to revise Articles of
Confederation.

1781   1786–1787   1787   L O A D I N G . . .

Weak central government
can't stop rebellions.

The rebellions worried leaders. They agreed that something had to be done. A stronger central government was needed. In 1787, the states sent **delegates** to a meeting in Philadelphia. Their task was to **revise** the Articles of Confederation. These men are often called **framers**.

State leaders talk about a new U.S. government.

LOADING...LOADING...LOADING...

Writing the Constitution

The delegates got to work on May 25. They studied the Articles of Confederation. It soon became clear—a new government was needed. This meant a new document. The framers began to plan. They worked in secret. They didn't want anyone to know what they were up to. Their plans could have caused more rebellions.

The Articles of Confederation create a weak central government.

Leaders from states meet to revise Articles of Confederation.

| 1781 | 1786–1787 | 1787 | MAY 25, 1787 |

Weak central government can't stop rebellions.

Delegates begin to work in secret.

Delegates meet at
Independence Hall to create
a new government.

The Articles of Confederation create a weak central government.

Leaders from states meet to revise Articles of Confederation.

Madison's "Virginia Plan" is read to the framers.

1781	1786–1787	1787	MAY 25, 1787	MAY 29, 1787

Weak central government can't stop rebellions.

Delegates begin to work in secret.

James Madison was a framer from Virginia. He believed in a strong national government. He wrote the "Virginia Plan." It formed a new government. This was a big step toward the Constitution. The plan was read to all the framers on May 29. It was the first plan proposed.

James Madison is called the "Father of the Constitution."

Madison's plan formed a new **federal** government. It divided power into three branches. The legislative branch would make the laws. The executive branch would enforce the laws. And the judicial branch would decide how the laws are applied. The plan also set up **checks and balances**. No branch would have too much power.

> **Madison's plan created the three branches of government we have today.**

The Articles of Confederation create a weak central government.

Leaders from states meet to revise Articles of Confederation.

Madison's "Virginia Plan" is read to the framers.

| 1781 | 1786–1787 | 1787 | MAY 25, 1787 | MAY 29, 1787 |

Weak central government can't stop rebellions.

Delegates begin to work in secret.

Madison's Plan

EXECUTIVE
carries out laws

FEDERAL GOVERNMENT

LEGISLATIVE
makes laws

JUDICIAL
evaluates laws

LOADING... LOADING... LOADING...

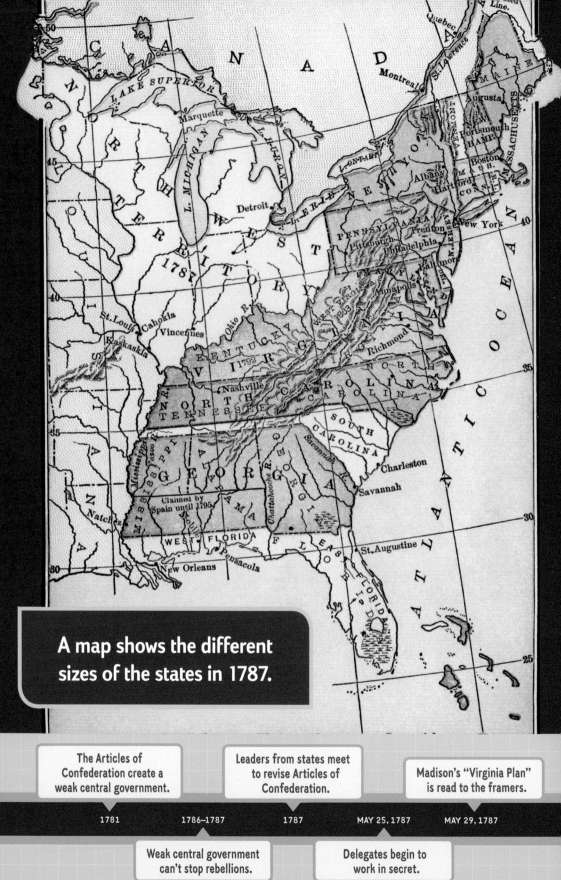

A map shows the different sizes of the states in 1787.

1781	1786–1787	1787	MAY 25, 1787	MAY 29, 1787

The Articles of Confederation create a weak central government.

Weak central government can't stop rebellions.

Leaders from states meet to revise Articles of Confederation.

Delegates begin to work in secret.

Madison's "Virginia Plan" is read to the framers.

Some framers didn't like Madison's plan. It favored big states, like Virginia. It gave states with more people more **representatives** in Congress. Framers from small states did not like this. In June 1787, framers from New Jersey proposed the "New Jersey Plan." In this plan, each state would have one vote in Congress. That way, every state had equal power.

The "New Jersey Plan" is proposed.

JUNE 15, 1787

LOADING... LOADING...

The framers debated. Tempers flared. In the end, they **compromised**. The legislative branch would have two chambers. One had two members from each state. This was the Senate. The other was the House. It would depend on a state's population. This was called "The Great Compromise."

The framers worked all summer. On September 17, 1787, the Constitution was signed.

The Articles of Confederation create a weak central government.

Leaders from states meet to revise Articles of Confederation.

Madison's "Virginia Plan" is read to the framers.

1781   1786–1787   1787   MAY 25, 1787   MAY 29, 1787

Weak central government can't stop rebellions.

Delegates begin to work in secret.

Framers from each state sign the Constitution.

The "New Jersey Plan" is proposed.

JUNE 15, 1787   SEPTEMBER 17, 1787

39 framers sign the Constitution.

The framers announce that the Constitution is written. It is off to the states to be ratified.

The Articles of Confederation create a weak central government.

Leaders from states meet to revise Articles of Confederation.

Madison's "Virginia Plan" is read to the framers.

1781   1786–1787   1787   MAY 25, 1787   MAY 29, 1787

Weak central government can't stop rebellions.

Delegates begin to work in secret.

Off to the States

Writing the Constitution was a huge job. But now the states had to **ratify** it. To become law, 9 of the 13 states had to vote to accept it. The states had meetings. Should they ratify the Constitution? It did not have a bill of rights. This worried some. They wanted their rights written down.

The "New Jersey Plan" is proposed.

JUNE 15, 1787   SEPTEMBER 17, 1787   DING . . . LOADING . . .

39 framers sign the Constitution.

Federalists wanted a strong federal government. They liked the Constitution as it was. Anti-federalists did not agree. They wanted a bill of rights. In the end, it was agreed to add a bill of rights. This would happen after the new government began. On June 21, 1788, the ninth state ratified the Constitution. It was law! It went into effect in March 1789.

The Constitution is law! People celebrate the new government with a parade.

The Articles of Confederation create a weak central government.		Leaders from states meet to revise Articles of Confederation.		Madison's "Virginia Plan" is read to the framers.
1781	1786–1787	1787	MAY 25, 1787	MAY 29, 1787
	Weak central government can't stop rebellions.		Delegates begin to work in secret.	

The "New Jersey Plan"
is proposed.

The ninth state ratifies
the Constitution.

JUNE 15, 1787   SEPTEMBER 17, 1787   JUNE 21, 1788   LOADING...

39 framers sign the
Constitution.

Women fight for the right to vote. The 19th Amendment, ratified in 1920, granted this right.

The Articles of Confederation create a weak central government.		Leaders from states meet to revise Articles of Confederation.		Madison's "Virginia Plan" is read to the framers.
1781	1786–1787	1787	MAY 25, 1787	MAY 29, 1787
	Weak central government can't stop rebellions.		Delegates begin to work in secret.	

Making Changes

The Constitution can be changed. These changes are called **amendments**. In 1791, the first 10 amendments were ratified. These make up the Bill of Rights. By 2018, there were 27 amendments. They all began in Congress. An amendment must pass with a two-thirds vote in the Senate and House. After that, three-fourths of the states must ratify it. Then it is added to the U.S. Constitution.

The "New Jersey Plan" is proposed.

The ninth state ratifies the Constitution.

JUNE 15, 1787   SEPTEMBER 17, 1787   JUNE 21, 1788   1791   ING . . .

39 framers sign the Constitution.

The first ten amendments—the Bill of Rights—are ratified.

The Constitution was written over 230 years ago. That's old! But it's still in effect today. Constitution Day is celebrated on September 17. That's the day the framers signed it. They made sure our Constitution could be changed. Amendments help our nation to be better. What will the next change be?

Americans enjoy the freedoms that are protected by the Constitution every day.

The Articles of Confederation create a weak central government.

Leaders from states meet to revise Articles of Confederation.

Madison's "Virginia Plan" is read to the framers.

1781   1786–1787   1787   MAY 25, 1787   MAY 29, 1787

Weak central government can't stop rebellions.

Delegates begin to work in secret.

The "New Jersey Plan" is proposed.

The ninth state ratifies the Constitution.

The Constitution is still the highest law of the United States.

| JUNE 15, 1787 | SEPTEMBER 17, 1787 | JUNE 21, 1788 | 1791 | TODAY |

39 framers sign the Constitution.

The first ten amendments—the Bill of Rights—are ratified.

Glossary

amendment A change to the U.S. Constitution. Amendments are added to the Constitution after they are passed by Congress and ratified by the states.

checks and balances A system that allows each branch of a government to check, or review, another branch's actions to prevent any one branch from having too much power.

compromise To give up something desired in order to get agreement.

delegate A person who represents a group or organization.

federal A system of government where states are united under one central power but also have their own government and can make their own laws.

federalist A person in favor of strong federal government.

framer A person who helped write the U.S. Constitution.

ratify To officially approve.

representative A person chosen to act or speak for others.

revise To make changes to something.

Read More

Barcella, Laura. *Know Your Rights!: A Modern Kid's Guide to the American Constitution.* New York: Sterling Children's Books, 2018.

Demuth, Patricia Brennan. *What is the Constitution?* New York: Penguin Workshop, 2018.

Small, Cathleen. *The Constitution: The Responsibilities and Powers of the U.S. Government.* New York: Lucent Press, 2018.

Websites

Ben's Guide—U.S. Constitution Facts and Figures
https://bensguide.gpo.gov/j-constitution-facts

BrainPOP | U.S. Constitution
https://www.brainpop.com/socialstudies/ushistory/usconstitution/

National Archives — The Constitution of the United States: A Transcription
https://www.archives.gov/founding-docs/constitution-transcript

Index

amendments 27, 28

Articles of Confederation 7, 11, 12

bill of rights 23, 24, 27

checks and balances 16

compromises 20

Constitution Day 28

federal government 16, 24

Great Britain 7

Madison, James 15, 16, 19

New Jersey Plan 19

Philadelphia 11

ratifying 23, 24, 27

rebellions 8, 11, 12

signing 20

Virginia Plan 15

writing 15, 23

About the Author

Matt Bowers is a writer and illustrator who lives in Minnesota. When he's not writing or drawing, he enjoys skiing, sailing, and going on adventures with his family. He hopes readers will continue to learn about government and be leaders in their communities.